Getting through Depression

"As children of God we don't have to be depressed or defeated in life."[1] Is this true? Did the person who wrote those words have his head in the sand, the clouds, or the Bible? Does having a heavenly Father guarantee a heavenly disposition? When we travel the high road with God, will we never plod the low one?

The issue is crucial. One counselor friend of mine says half of his patients come to him because they are depressed. It is, in fact, the most common kind of abnormal behavior. Each of us has a one in ten chance of becoming severely depressed. And all of us have our regular skirmishes with its milder form.

Depression is a complicated matter. Experts are not agreed on what causes it. And getting over it is not simply a matter of "picking yourself up" or "snapping out of it." We simply do not have all the answers, and we should be very careful about offering "easy formulas" or "pat solutions" for such a complex reality.

Becoming a Christian is not a vaccination against depression. Christianity does not equal happiness. The church is not Gladsville. True, Christians are urged to rejoice. Yet Christian joy can sometimes be mixed with cheerless despondency. The apostle Peter knew Christians could experience joy and grief at the same time. "In this you greatly rejoice, even though now for a little while, if necessary, you have been distressed by various trials" (1 Peter 1:6 NASB).

Many Christians don't seem to think that way. As a fairly new Christian, I remember being surprised when my theology professor said: "Sometimes when you feel down, you don't need to pray more, you need a good night's sleep." His statement popped a guilt-filled balloon inside me. Somehow I had gotten the idea that I ought always to be "up."

Jesus, our example, was understandably "exceedingly sorrowful, even to the point of death," prior to His crucifixion. And down through the centuries many famous godly people have had noble bouts with mournful depression.

"My soul is downcast," said the weeping prophet, Jeremiah (Lamentations 3:20).

David complained: "My eyes grow weak with sorrow, my soul and my body with grief" (Psalm 31:9).

Martin Luther graphically described one of his frequent rock-bottom moods: "For more than a week I was close to the gates of death and hell. I trembled in all my members. Christ was wholly lost. I was shaken by desperation and blasphemy of God."[2]

Depression's victims include famous preacher Charles Spurgeon, Christian author C. S. Lewis, and poet Amy Carmichael.

The plight of Job, among the most notable sufferers, is the theme of the oldest book of the Bible. Job had plenty to sink his heart. In rapid succession he lost family, wealth, and health. After his wife advised, "Curse God and die," Job slipped quickly into a deep pit of despair.

Job's Depression Test

Job's descriptions of despair are so accurate that you can use them to test your own emotional state. You can check yourself by marking the appropriate items.

Extreme sadness. "Why is light given to him who suffers, and life to the bitter of soul?" (3:20 NASB). Which is true of you? (a) I don't feel sad. (b) I am somewhat sad. (c) I am sad all the time and can't get over it. (d) I am so sad I am not sure I can stand it.

Sleep disturbance. "When I lie down I say, 'When shall I arise?' But the night continues, and I am continually tossing until dawn" (7:4 NASB). Questions: (a) I do not find myself becoming more tired than usual. (b) I get tired more easily than I used to. (c) I get tired doing almost anything. (d) I am too tired to do anything.

Pessimism about life. "Man, who is born of woman, is shortlived and full of turmoil" (14:1 NASB). (a) I am not particularly discouraged about the future. (b) I feel discouraged about the future. (c) I feel I have nothing to look forward to. (d) I feel the future is hopeless and that things cannot improve.

Life seems worthless. "I do not take notice of myself; I despise my life" (9:21 NASB). (a) I get as much satisfaction out of things as I used to. (b) I don't enjoy things the way I used to. (c) I don't get real satisfaction out of anything anymore. (d) I am dissatisfied or bored with everything.

Helplessness. "I am not at ease, nor am I quiet, and I am not at rest, but turmoil comes" (3:26 NASB). (a) I don't cry any more than usual. (b) I cry more now than I used to. (c) I cry all the time now. (d) I used to be able to cry, but now I can't cry even though I want to.

Physical signs of sadness. "My eye has also grown dim because of grief, and all my members are as a shadow" (17:7 NASB). (a) My appetite is no worse than normal. (b) My appetite is not as good as it used to be. (c) My appetite is much worse now. (d) I have no appetite at all.

(a) I have not noticed any recent change in my interest in sex. (b) I am less interested in sex than I used to be. (c) I am much less interested in sex now. (d) I have lost interest in sex completely.

Desire for death. "Who long for death, but there is none, and dig for it more than for hidden treasures" (3:21 NASB). (a) I don't have thoughts of killing myself. (b) I have thoughts of killing myself, but I would not carry them out. (c) I would like to kill myself. (d) I would kill myself if I had the chance.[3]

Depression may also be marked by feelings of failure, lack of satisfaction, irritation, and loss of interest in people. This brief self check, however, is not intended to be absolutely accurate. It might signal you need to see a trained counselor and should not be used to replace going to one.

If you marked a lot of items with "a's" and a few "b's," depression is certainly not on your doorstep. If, however, you have a number of "c's" and a "d" or two, you have entered some sort of dark tunnel. A recent happening might explain it: a death of a loved one, the loss of a job or a friend. But if your glum mood begs for explanation, it is important for you to talk to a counselor. If you have any serious thought about taking your life, it is urgent that you talk with someone. And in the event that someone has confided to you thoughts about suicide, consider it an emergency—get them to help now.

From time to time we have all had a lack of energy, a negative self-image, a sense of hopelessness, and other signs of depression. We can usually point to a clear-cut cause: recovery from an illness, exhaustion from hard work, a loss. These symptoms are part of grieving.

It may be normal to be in an emotional cellar even when some sobering event didn't shove you there. Depression can accompany a physical illness. A simple lack of exercise may be the culprit. And for many women, regular monthly blue periods are due to the menstrual cycle.

We can, however, distinguish between these so-called "normal," temporary bouts and depressive illness. By no means is the difference completely clear. Apparently there are some common elements in each. The "lows" are similar in three ways:

1. The descriptions of the negative feelings are much the same: sadness, loneliness, and feelings of unworthiness.

2. The behavior of one matches the other: withdrawal from activity, weakness, and diminished sexual interest.

3. The physical reactions are similar: insomnia, fatigue, and loss of appetite.

Yet it is possible to tell one from the other. Normal depression does not incapacitate. That is, a person doesn't get to the place where he or she cannot work and fulfill expected responsibilities. This doesn't mean that the "normally" depressed might not be able to work for a time. We don't expect a grieving person to take up full responsibilities right away. But whenever an individual is not pulling his weight at a time when he should reasonably be expected to do so, something beyond the "normal" is happening.

Times of normal depression are also brief. Severe grieving usually lasts for a few months, though some internal sadness can continue for years. If extreme distress continues much longer than these few months—and seems to be getting worse—the sufferer may have a depressive illness.

One other distinguishing mark: the normally down-hearted retain a grasp on reality. They can usually experience and admit to some joy and beauty along with their moments of depression. Depressive illnesses, on the other hand, may plunge someone into such horrible darkness that the bleakness distorts their whole view of life. Looking back, one victim described the agony: "It was a horror and hell. I was at the bottom of the deepest pit there ever was. I was worthless and unforgivable. I was as good as—no, worse than—dead."[4]

When I was a young man, I tried to counsel with a woman in that state. Her shoulders drooped, her hands hung helplessly at her sides or else nervously twisted at her handkerchief. Deep, dark crescents under her eyes accented her melancholy look. Not understanding the extent of her illness, I tried to reason with her. "God has not forsaken you," I pleaded. "You are not damned as you now suspect." The positive, beautiful statements of God's grace and love from Scripture seemed incapable of penetrating her darkness as she cowered in the chair in the corner of the room.

There was no reasoning with her. I could not point to facts and wholesome, uplifting ideas. To her, reality was a distorted gloom that tormented her and twisted her perception of life. Electroshock therapy lasting over a period of weeks made her see clearly once again. She was able to take hope from God's Word and the encouragement of loved ones.

Depressive illnesses are severe and life threatening.[5] According to Christian physician John White, they may take one of several forms:

Secondary depression. Depression that arises in the course of illness, or from conditions such as alcoholism, homosexuality, diabetes, and Cushing's syndrome. Remember there is usually some depression accompanying any injury or illness. It is the most common emotional response for both children and adults, often coming a few days after the injury or the onset of illness. When healing or recovery is slow or delayed, depression may set in.

Primary depression. This mood disorder cannot be associated with any other form of mental or physical illness. However, because we don't fully understand all of the relationships between physical illness and depression, it is difficult to make a distinction between primary and secondary depression.

Bipolar depression. These are primary depressions which are characterized not only by plunges into despair, but also by ascents into euphoria and even wild excitement.

Unipolar depression. These depressions do not combine highs and lows, but, as their name suggests, are plunges into darkness relieved only by normal moods.[6]

It would seem that depression, a condition so highly visible, ought to have a cause that is just as obvious. But this just isn't so. Cast a net out over the entire history of thinking about depression and you'll bring in numerous ideas about what's behind it.

It's crucial to look at these in an effort to understand depression. But it isn't always necessary to know the cause to prescribe a treatment. Depressive symptoms may be treated and vanish before anyone can pinpoint a cause.

Many of the following "causes" go a long way toward explaining both normal and severe depression. Just examining them might give you a clue to what gives you the blahs now and then. You might also gain some insight into the reasons for the depressive state of someone you're concerned about.[7]

Anger. It is common to think of depression as a form of anger turned inward. First introduced by Sigmund Freud, this theory is no longer adequate to explain serious depressive illness. It may account, however, for the so-called "normal" depressed mood we sometimes have.

When we get upset with someone we love, respect, or are afraid of, we may not *allow* ourselves to be angry with them. Perhaps the one stirring our ire is our spouse; we're afraid turning loose our anger will turn him or her away. Or the agitator could be a boss or relative. Showing our wrath might threaten to bring his down on us. Perhaps guilt, not fear, keeps our anger in. We don't accept the rightfulness of anger. Or we simply can't justify being angry with someone we ought to love (as in the case of a teenager upset by a parent).

When the anger is kept in, it is sometimes *turned* in. The flow of bad feelings gushes back into our lives, like water streaming from a broken pipe. In short, we blame ourselves and end up feeling down about self, about life, and about the future. We feel lonely, sad, blue, guilty, and sometimes even lost and empty. And we often can't figure out why.

The despondency may very well melt away when we work it out or talk it out. It will fade even more quickly when we admit to ourselves we are mad at someone and handle it. Unadmitted anger is uncontrolled anger. Facing up to it is one way to get rid of it.

Loss. Bereavement can cause brief depression but can also trigger a depressive illness. What seems like a normal response becomes prolonged until the person is in a hopeless, helpless condition.

Why this happens to some people is not absolutely certain. John White claims a lot of evidence proves previous losses can make a person "depressive prone." A traumatic event sends them into a nose dive. A person who has lost a parent in childhood, for instance, may be more susceptible to depression in adulthood. Studies show that some persons (especially women) who are depression prone came from homes where parents fought a great deal.[8]

Inconsistent parental love can also be a factor. It is possible that these people grew up with a fear of traumatic detachment from parents which makes them susceptible to an onslaught of serious depression. We know parental affection in life's early years seems to contribute a great deal to later mental and emotional stability. When growing up we need to feel close to people and sense we belong. Early childhood experiences that make us feel neglected or rejected may not always cause depression in adulthood. However, being deprived of normal affection from parents and others might make a person prone to depression. Experts call this a "predisposing cause."

Old age. Depression is one of the most common complaints of the aged. Since older people endure so many losses, their depression is most likely a normal grief response, not an illness. Since aging itself does not cause depression, older persons with emotional disturbances should be treated like other age groups. Too often counseling is withheld from the elderly because they are thought to be incurable. Physicians may be inclined to treat them with drugs, believing the only goal is to give them an illusion of normalcy until they die. These drugs, often with harmful side effects, should not substitute for some attempt to help the older person cope with his moods and circumstances.

Loss of self-esteem. An exaggerated negative, punitive view of oneself is a symptom of depression. "Wretched, useless, helpless," are among the words the mirthless fling at themselves. Is this lack of self-esteem a cause of depression? Some experts think so. The feeling of helplessness and the loss of self-worth come first; the sadness and other gloom symptoms follow. The damaged self-respect usually comes when a person is unable to reach cherished ideals or goals. Naturally, this can be related to a loss. The lost job may mean one will never achieve his vocational goals. Or a lost loved one may trigger the sense of failure—a person may blame himself for the death. Or if he doesn't hold up well afterward, he may be severely disappointed with himself.

Because this guilt and lack of self-esteem are associated with depression, some people blame religion for contributing to the problem. From religion one may get unrealistic ideals, a low view of self, a strong concept of the necessity of punishment, and little assurance of forgiveness. Together they could cause depression. One counselor refers to this as "worm theology."[9] He points to lyrics of hymns to make his case: "such a worm as I," "wretch like me," "coming weak and vile," "poor, wretched, blind," "guilty, vile and helpless we."

No doubt this accusation contains some truth. Some Christians may not have enough exposure to the grace and love of God. Sin and failure lead them to collapse in depressive self-hatred. Misguided Christians may begin to equate sinfulness with worthlessness. They need to be reminded that all people are created in God's image. Scripture affirms that men and women are sinful, but it also affirms that we are not junk. Each individual is incalculably important to the Creator.

Sometimes Christians fall prey to false guilt. The individual continues to condemn himself for some wrong even when God has forgiven. It may very well be that nothing was done to require forgiveness in the first place.

The critical spirit of other Christians sometimes makes it difficult. Paul Tournier suggests that this pressure to "please others" is a basic factor in the creation of false guilt. True guilt comes from reproachment by God in our inner heart for sins we have committed. False guilt comes from judgments made by others—judgments which may or may not reflect the thoughts of God. The Bible is an all-important guide to the Christian in distinguishing between true and false guilt.[10]

It also helps to realize that *guilt may come from sources other than God.* Society, self, and Satan can induce it. The apostle Paul claims false prophets send people on guilt trips. Those who make unreasonable demands are said to give "attention to deceitful spirits and doctrines of demons" (1 Timothy 4:1 NASB). This fits the biblical notion that Satan is an accuser of the brethren (Revelation 12:10).

Ask several questions to distinguish false from real guilt:

1. Can I trace my feelings to some disobedience against the clear teachings of Scripture?

2. Do my feelings relate in many ways to my past experiences as a child?

3. Do my guilt feelings persist after I have made a confession of my sin?

4. Are my feelings related to some unrealistic standards or goals I have set for myself?

5. Do I fear giving up my feelings of guilt? (Sometimes if we fail to feel guilty, we fear we may fail to achieve our goals. Such feelings of guilt are not the highest motivation for growing in the Christian life.)[11]

Sometimes we must let go of unrealistic standards that are beating us down and exchange less achievement for more peace of mind.

The theory that depression is caused by a lack of self-esteem has the chicken-egg problem. Is lack of self-worth the *cause* or the *symptom* of depression? Experts who deal with the severely depressed know that dealing with the guilt itself can be futile. The dark, dank mood swallows up arguments, Scripture verses, and other assurances of God's favor. Something else is causing the depression. When the bad mood goes away the good self-view will follow.

Hopelessness. Believing in mind over matter, some psychologists say depression is a problem with the mind, not the mood. The depressed person thinks too negatively about self, the present, and the future. Hopelessness sets in whenever that mindset occurs.

Change the mind, they say, and it will change the emotional state. This approach, called "rational therapy," has a lot to commend it, and has proven effective for many people. The treatment, however, is not as simple as it sounds. Rational therapists use numerous methods to treat the depressed; it's not merely a matter of telling persons to shape up or talking them into a good view of life.

Anxiety. Depression, pure and simple, is a problem of being human. Life in general generates anxiety. Living becomes threatening or meaningless.

Perhaps there is more depression today because personal reasons for existence do not spring easily from modern life. We are bombarded by a confusing array of viewpoints which are devoid of any awareness of God. Without God and without hope is a cheerless state to be in. Add to this the everyday stresses and the threat of nuclear holocaust. In this, Jesus offers hope: "Be of good cheer, I have overcome the world."

Brain chemistry. Just recently, psychologists have been made aware of the role of neurochemical balance in explaining and treating depression. It is quite clear that chemical changes in the brain occur simultaneously with depressive illness. But it is not clear that this is depression's cause. The question "which influences which?" is still unanswered.[12]

Brain chemistry is complex, as is the brain itself. The number of brain cells in each human equals the number of stars in our galaxy, about one hundred million. Communication has to go on between those cells. Sometimes the signals between them don't get through very well. Different things can go wrong. One of these hindrances has to do with the sodium chloride content within the cell. Because this salt plays a part in messages getting from cell to cell, something breaks down whenever the sodium ions and the chloride ions get out of balance. Sometimes the chemical problem is in another part of the cell.

Whenever there is a slowdown of cellular communication, memory and concentration can be affected. The transmitter problem, however, causes more trouble than this. It affects other glands of the body, making the overall condition a whole body chemistry matter.

Enormous numbers of people have been helped by doses of lithium (an inert salt) because it brings the sodium chloride back into balance. Certain antidepressant medications are used to treat other chemistry problems.

Demon possession. It's not hard to see how the gloom and doom aspects of depression can be closely associated with evil spiritual powers. Persons often feel as though they are in the grip of something they can't shake. When you see how helpless and tormented a dejected person sometimes is, it is very easy to suspect some lurking supernatural power is at work in them.

Because the New Testament confirms the reality of demon possession and oppression, demons can't be ruled out as a cause of depression. Contemporary Christians tell us of encounters with such cases.

But we must be cautious—extremely cautious—about labeling someone as "demon-possessed." What might initially appear to be a convenient diagnosis could turn out to be complicating—and damaging. Other causes ought to be first considered. Suppose a depression is induced by chemical changes or emotional turmoil? Efforts to cast out a demon will fail. The despondent person may be driven into greater depths of hopelessness when a supposed "demon" will not leave despite the prayers and efforts of Christian friends.

Blaming depression on a demon may not lead to an easy solution. Christ's apostles failed to cast out a demon on one embarrassing occasion. Some of these beings are apparently quite stubborn and powerful. Jesus identified the one that resisted the disciples as the kind that comes out "only by prayer" (Mark 9:14-29).

Whether or not we know the cause of a loved one's depression, we can still pray for his health. When his condition becomes severe, no matter whether we suspect demon activity or not, we should seek the help of a competent Christian psychologist.

Treating Depression

It should be apparent by now that just as there is no one cause of depression, there will be no single treatment. Persons with depressive illnesses will not respond to being told to "snap out of it." Getting them to a competent professional counselor will be the kindest thing we can do for them.

The following suggestions are applicable to our normal, mild depressions as well as the more serious ones. Please note, however, that they may do little good for someone who is in a very low state. I offer these simply as potentially helpful guidelines. I have no intention of guaranteeing they will automatically lead everyone through the tunnel of gloom.

Getting the picture. See depression for what it is. When depressed, we picture ourselves in a "pit" or "black hole." We talk about "being down" and "going down." Why not think of it as a *tunnel*? Depression may not be something to climb out of as much as something to "go through."

Like a tunnel, as soon as you enter depression, you are already on the way out. You may just be at the beginning. That's the bad news. But the good news is that you'll get through it. You'll see the light again.

For this reason, experts tell us depression can be good for us. It is a normal response to certain circumstances of life.

We *should* mourn when we sin. Sadness is a positive response to committing a crime or hurting someone. Those who don't know sorrow cannot say, "I'm sorry."

When crisis or loss crash into our lives, depression may be beneficial. Slowed down, we process our thoughts and reexamine our perspectives and values. Depression gives the feelings the chance to respond, to regroup, and to do whatever emotions do to heal themselves. Depression is a healing process, or, perhaps, the pain that the healing process generates. It is ultimately put to good use and becomes a source of personal growth.[13]

Despite the torment of his dark periods, Luther said, "Without them no man can understand Scripture, faith, the fear or the love of God."[14]

This does not mean that we nurture our depression. But it does mean that in some respects we can't fight it. Beating at it, frantically waving one's arms at the black vapor within the soul as if to drive it out, will not work.

What then do we do with depression? We live with it, doing what we can to eventually make it lift.

Beware the easy quick fix. Despondency can make us desperate. We grasp for any promising cure. It is easy to believe that something that worked for someone else will work for us. If we pray a certain prayer, the heaviness will lift. If we do a certain thing, relief will come.

We hear about people who seemed to find simple solutions and sudden, almost miraculous relief. We want the same. Several days ago I read about a pastor whose depression cost him his job and hospitalized him. After release from the hospital he went alone to a mountain cabin to think and pray. Meditation and Scripture convinced him his problem was related to a spiritual battle with Satan.

"Oh, God," he sobbed, "is this what is happening to me?" He told God he had ignored His help in overcoming his depression. Then, it happened. "I noticed as I remained there that things felt different," he recollected. "Nothing ecstatic or noisy. Nothing high-powered or sensational. I just felt different. As I examined that feeling, I became aware of the strength in my limbs, of objects before my eyes. I saw, I felt, I heard. Was it possible? Was the cloud finally gone? Had my world come alive again? I began thanking and praising God, singing and laughing."

He returned home a new man. In a few days his family was telling everyone: "Dad is finally out of his black hole. Dad's depression is gone."[15]

Reading this, a depressed person might easily think the same thing could happen to him. A simple prayer. A realization. A confession. A few days in a mountain cabin. It worked for him—maybe it will work for me.

The man who wrote that account would not want anyone to think that. He tells of the months of counseling, the weeks of hospitalization that were a prelude to his mountain cabin experience. Perhaps some new realization turned the corner for him. Nevertheless, all of the previous agonizing, counseling, and hospitalization may have been necessary before the healing finally came. The mountain-top experience was only the last dose in the treatment . . . not the only one.

Share the load. Studies confirm that people who have someone to confide in are better able to handle life's stresses. Depression thrives on your keeping it to yourself. Admitting to others your honest feelings keeps you honest with yourself. It helps you think better and somehow opens holes to let out some of the gloom.

Grasp the feeling/thought connection. All parts of us are connected: body, emotions, and thoughts. Each acts on the other. The physical self can make the emotional self feel down, as everyone who has had the common cold knows. Likewise the emotional self can affect the mental self, making the mind churn out all kinds of ridiculous things. When depressed, Luther thought terrible things about God. In grief, C. S. Lewis tells how he pictured God as some sort of monster.

When our feelings are drooping we should realize that they are probably telling the mind what to think. Statements like "I am no good" or "I can't do anything right" or "God could never forgive *my* sin" aren't really what the intellect is saying. It is what the emotions are telling it to think. Negative feelings give birth to negative thoughts. We can't take these thoughts seriously.

When depression becomes an illness, a person is unable to control these thoughts and mistakenly takes them at face value. He loses touch with reality. It does little good to appeal to a person's thoughts when they have succumbed to the control of their dreary, morose feelings. Treatment with antidepressants or other therapy may be needed to transform the emotions and change the thoughts.

But this doesn't mean that we should stop reasoning and talking sense with depressed persons. We can work at generating right thinking.

While feelings can control our thoughts, it can be the other way around. We need to utilize our spiritual and mental resources when we are down. Fill the mind with positive thoughts even though the emotions are saying, "That's baloney."

Words about hope, grace, love, and forgiveness may not immediately pop us into heavenly sunshine. But the input is significant in the long run. Good music can soothe the feelings while cheerful lyrics can stimulate the mind.

Get the body moving. Action can be like medicine. Emotions respond to circumstances even when they don't heed our thoughts. Emotions are rebellious at times. They won't take orders. They easily ignore commands such as "Stop being angry" or "Don't feel sad" or "Be happy."

Nevertheless, our *will* can handle emotions when the thoughts can't. When we feel blue, we can ask our will to do something about it. "Will," we can say, "take the body out where there is a chance the emotions will start feeling better."

Psychologist William James maintained that our emotions are closely connected to our actions. We are afraid, he would say, because we are acting frightened. We've all experienced this at the swimming pool. As we lie in the sun, our emotions aren't up to a jump into that cold water. We may try without success to convince our emotions to rise to the occasion. But then "will" takes over. We jump into the water and start swimming. Suddenly we *feel* like swimming. William James would explain, that you feel like swimming because you are doing it. That reverses the usual notion: that we swim because we feel like it.

To paraphrase James, we would help ourselves out of depression by doing nondepressive things—even if we don't feel like doing them.

Martin Luther also suggested some down-to-earth cures for depression. He advised people with mild bouts to ignore the heaviness. Luther counseled sufferers to shun solitude and seek the warm company of friends, discussing irrelevant matters. "A good way to exorcise the Devil," he maintained, "was to harness the horse and spread manure on the fields."[16]

Physical exercise seems to be a universal treatment for depression, no matter how severe that depression may be. Granted, the thought of jogging around the block may make someone more depressed. But it is important to begin doing something to get the heart and blood and muscles working. Even with a short walk, you will get started toward more walking. And that's progress.

Perhaps one of the reasons physical exercise works so well is that it gives a person some control over his life and circumstances. One of the marks of depression is a morbid fear about the helplessness of the situation. The future seems bleak; nothing can be done to change the present. This attitude needs to be changed. Doing something that makes you feel in control is a way of doing that.

A psychologist treats the depressed by helping them consider what project they would like to undertake. Sometimes they want to do something about the weight they've gained. Starting an exercise program and a diet can be a step toward regaining the sense of mastery that seems to be lost. This becomes the first step out of the pit.

Exercise three-way trust. What does confronting depression mean for the believer? Does it mean "facing it" or "*faithing* it"? If Scripture says the just shall live by faith, it implies that the depressed will get through by faith. Not that practical and even medical treatments are unnecessary. It's just that these should be undergirded and upheld by trust in a faithful God.

1. Trust means relying on God's power rather than on our strength. "Our competence comes from God" (2 Corinthians 3:4). There is relief for those who "take their hands off their own lives and fall into God's arms." No matter how you got into the tunnel, let God bring you out.

2. Trust means relying on God's mercy and grace. "For it is by grace you have been saved, through faith," Scripture reminds us, "and this not from yourselves, it is the gift of God—it is not by works" (Ephesians 2:8-9). This is a radical

thought. It means that I did nothing to make God love me. Therefore, I can do nothing to make Him love me more. And I can do nothing wrong to make Him love me less. Committed to a Savior who died for our sins, we can rely on God's grace.

3. Trust means hoping. Contemplating his own depressed heart, the psalmist asked himself, "Why are you downcast, O my soul? Why so disturbed within me?" Without waiting for an answer, he told himself: "Put your hope in God" (Psalm 42:5).

Once my wife, Ginger, showed me a verse of Scripture that had helped carry her through a few years ago. We were delightfully astonished. Without her knowing it, I too had found that same statement of Scripture and was often turning it over in my mind during the same period of distress. It was Psalm 30:5: "Weeping may remain for a night, but rejoicing comes in the morning."

This thought may not stop our weeping. It may not sweep away our despair. *But it can make us weep and despair in hope.* There is a morning ahead.

The severely depressed man I mentioned earlier found this out. Joyless, dejected, he eventually sprawled on the carpet in his office. Don Baker was hopelessly unable to face even the simplest task. His helpless wife admitted him to a hospital psychiatric ward. At the time, he felt nothing positive, saw no bright spot. After doctors examined him one of them said some gentle words—words Baker later said he would always be grateful for.

"Mr. Baker, you are deeply depressed—you need help—but you'll get better. It will take time

. . . but you'll get better."[17]

Hope is not just the light at the end of the tunnel of gloom. It is the one sure light in the darkest part of it.

You'll get through.

---

[1]Bob George, "There's No Need to Be Depressed," *Moody Monthly*, February, 1982, p. 7.

[2] In Roland Bainton, *Here I Stand* (Nashville: Abingdon, 1950), p. 36.

[3]Questions are adapted from Becks Inventory for Measuring Depression (University of Pennsylvania Press, 1967).

[4]In John Altrocchi, *Abnormal Behavior* (New York: Harcourt Brace Jovanovich, 1980), p. 56.

[5]John White, *The Masks of Melancholy* (Downers Grove, Ill.: InterVarsity Press, 1982), p. 62.

[6]White, *Masks of Melancholy*, p. 63.

[7]T. McKinney, "Overview of Recent Research in Depression: Integration of Ten Conceptual Models into a Comprehensive Clinical Frame," *Archives* 32 (1975): 285-305; and "Depressive Disorders: Toward a Unified Hypothesis," *Science* 182 (October 1974): 20-29. In White, *Masks of Melancholy*, pp. 104-140.

[8]*Journal of Abnormal Psychology*, vol. 88, no. 4 (1979): 398-406.

[9]Dwight W. Cumbee, "Depression as an Ecclesiogenic Neurosis," *The Journal of Pastoral Care*, vol. XXXIV, no. 4 (December 1980), p. 259.

[10]Paul Tournier, *Guilt and Grace* (New York: Harper & Row, 1962), p. 67.

[11]Lloyd M. Perry and Charles M. Sell, *Speaking to Life's Problems* (Chicago: Moody Press, 1983), pp. 146-147.

[12]Richard E. Keady, "Depression, Psychophysiology and Concepts of God," *Encounter* 41: 265 (Summer 1980).

[13]Keady, "Depression," p. 265.

[14]Smiley Blanton, *Love or Perish* (New York: Simon and Schuster, (1956), pp. 36.

[15]Don Baker and Emery Nester, *Depression: Finding Hope and Meaning in Life's Darkest Shadow* (Portland, Oreg.: Multnomah Press, 1983), pp. 101-103.

[16]Bainton, *Here I Stand*, p. 364.

[17]Baker and Nester, *Depression*, p. 20.